Husband Material Volume I:
Stories From The Streets

All Poems Written by D. L. Husband
Copyright © 2024
All Rights Reserved
Published by
DEADMAN'S PRESS INK, ALBANY NY

All work is intellectual property of the author in perpetuity.
All artwork belongs to the artists in perpetuity.
Consent has been granted for use of art by the artist(s) in this book in all forms.

'I'd be a savage beast; if I didn't have this outlet to salvage me inside'
(Eminem, 2005)

This is the last time I will apologise for my past.

My dedications...

First and foremost, to the streets. You chewed me up and spat me out cleaner than most. Could've been brown bread. Could've been toast. But, like it or not, you taught me the most.

For better, for worse. Despite of, because of.

Secondly, I'd like to thank my wishbone. My funny bone. My Emily...you stood by me when things were hardest. Helped me when things were darkest. Loved me and trusted me when I gave you every reason not to. Now, here you are, getting a mention in the same dream you are always pushing me towards. 'I love you all of it.'

After that, I'd like to thank the Husbands, Hoggs, Dobbies, Whitmores and Shaws. The family; you've all taught me something. The Bones, Heaths and Tervitts; you all taught me something too.

Friends old and new, long gone and yet to come. One for the living and one for the dead. To those who've helped me along the way, you have my deepest and most humble gratitude and thanks.

Also, huge thanks to Christopher Parkin (@christophski) for providing the artwork for each of the section cover pages.

Lastly, to my younger self. Thank you for not giving up, no matter how shit things got. Keep laughing. Keep moving. Keep it unapologetically you. Love ya, kid.

Every day is a school day: lessons, lessons. *Lessons.*

HUMBLED. HUNGRY. SINCERELY. HUSBAND.

Contents

Foreword
pg. 8

Part I: The Caterpillar
pg. 11

Intermission
pg. 36

Part II: The Chrysalis
pg. 38

Intermission II
pg. 65

Part III: The Butterfly
pg. 68

Afterword
pg. 87

Index
pg. 91

HUSBAND MATERIAL VOL. 1: STORIES FROM THE STREETS

A COLLECTION OF POETRY AND PROSE
BY D.L. HUSBAND

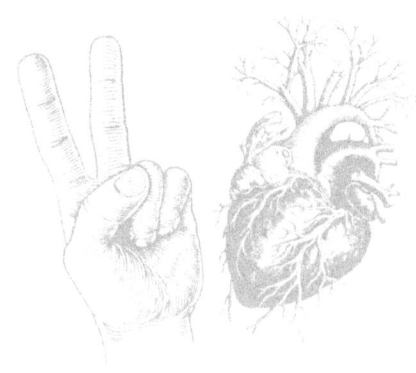

"The man who moves a mountain begins by carrying away small stones."

Confucius

"When we meet real tragedy in life, we can react in two ways – either by losing hope and falling into self-destructive habits, or by using the challenge to find our inner strength.

Dalai Lama

"Words have energy and power with the ability to help, to heal, to hinder, to hurt, to harm, to humiliate, and to humble."

Yehuda Berg

Foreword

My love for the written word started when I was very young. I read many books throughout my life, from Mr. Men to Mr. Nice, Plato to Kano and I feel I can associate with the latter, see that vision, and split between the philosopher and the streets; perhaps that's where they all come from.

I've lived in the Northeast of England all my life. I've seen enough of life to know you must take the good in front of you, try to negate the negatives you can, because so much of this life is out of our control.

My Father had a stroke when I was eleven years old and passed away when I was a young man of twenty-three; this had a significant impact on me and still has to this day, leading me to spiral into a drink and drug fueled decade of instability, homelessness, and crime.

When I was homeless, I stayed in a halfway house, a place designed to house the detritus this society leaves in its wake. My father worked there when I was a child and I vividly remember visiting: walking through the gates that first day as an adult, at what I thought was probably my lowest point. It nearly consumed me.

Consumption has been a constant crutch to me. Like a sorrow-filled caterpillar, I fed and fed on everything good in my life until there was nothing left but skeletal leaves that were once blossoming relationships, creating chaos where there was nothing but opportunity for growth and renewal.

It has been a hard pattern to break. I'm still working on it, but I write this: sixty days sober. I've never done this long without alcohol and hard drugs since I was sixteen years old. With this newfound sobriety has come waves of emotional reconciliation and memories of earth-shattering trauma, joyous love and all that exists in between, in the foggy and forgotten lands that are each of our pasts.
During the process of putting this manuscript together I have found a cathartic determination. I see how much reference and relevance there is in some themes discussed and how they directly link to raw emotions and stages of the life I have lived. Conflict and loss. Betrayal and deception. Love and hope.

Weathering storms and surviving through the nights. I hope you find something unexpected in here.

Unexpected gifts are always the best.

> 'The presence is a present'
> (Winnie the Pooh).

Whilst we can't ever know our futures, be they ordained by a divine power, a matter of simple cause and effect or whichever myriad of designs the human mind applies to our lives, know this... live a life that allows love to be available and true to yourself and to others. Seeing some of the things I have seen and doing some of the things I've done in my life so far have left me, as I'm sure many of us have been, at a loss with myself. I just didn't have the words for the pain, but I've found certain metaphors and imagery really provided me with a frame to build on.

Perhaps I do have the words, now.

Perhaps I have all along. We shall see. The pieces of me I'm about to share I have written over the last decade. Here is my poetic roller coaster. A tribute to all that has come before, that is now, and that will be. One for the dead and one for the living. We can't remain lost forever. In these words, I hope we can find some redemption, together.

PART I -
THE CATERPILLAR

"I have absolutely no pleasure in the stimulants in which I sometimes so madly indulge. It has not been in the pursuit of pleasure that I have periled life and reputation and reason. It has been the desperate attempt to escape from torturing memories, from a sense of insupportable loneliness and a dread of some strange impending doom."

Edgar Allen Poe

"Light thinks it travels faster than anything, but it is wrong. No matter how fast light travels, it finds the darkness has always got there first, and is waiting for it."

Terry Pratchett, Reaper Man

"I'm living everyday like a hustle, another drug to juggle. Another day, another struggle."

Biggie Smalls

Overachieving Disbeliever
_(2013)_

Today we received, overachieved and I see yet, we still disbelieve in our own perfection, our own self-perception, our own relationships, or our bitter rejections. See, I am me and you are you, and we are both beings just floating through. A wave, which in time, fades like the dew under the solar rays which warm the bones of me/you. So, now where to? I guess, to the view, the one that reminds of the real you of you, be that a single place, a memory or granny's stew, the subjectivity is all up to, who?

Wish I was through but only just beginning. I'll limit all the sinning, bullshit, and drug dealing. Forgot how to fight when I learned how to love because love's the universe. A single man is a thug, a man with no mind or desperate situation, created by his own disastrous animation. But life ain't no Tyson, no Frazier or Ali, it's all those motherfuckers' times three, and behind me, swinging through, with a right hook that's true, all you see is the tweety birds, like old school cartoons.

Life can be a beating, a lesson, or a dream. Remember lazy days floating down the stream, weather supreme, where's me strawberries and cream? Then autumn ticks in and takes a kick at me. September 13th, a little part of my sea escaped through clasped hands, prayer, and revelry.

I guess funerals and wakes are only for those left, with a bitter farewell alas, I digress.

Lest we forget, there are times that will test, so reset, for your best is yet to beset. I live and learn, yet to procreate but I promise you all, idiocy I'll sate in my kids, plenty knowledge on their plate, food in their bellies and manners by the crate.

Tough enough to look life in the face, give it a little laugh, and be on their way.
I wish the virtuous, the honest and the just could use just an ounce of that bravery they've got, because the said states of being, a coward can't hold a torch to because, snap, the light beholds the cowards' mirth, the haters words of hurt, and all the disbelievers throwing the foulest curse words.

But really, words, you'd think that'd beat me? Fuck! I've surpassed people life itself defeated, depleted and eaten, swallowed whole or chewed up. Versions of themselves or merely memories dreamed of, and yet I've looked at me and probably looked at you.

One two, three, let's say it together, rolling dice on the mirror, fuck, there ain't a lot better, cos with that analysis, you blaze away the spirits, the haunting Deja Entendu.

Ok, so blame me, for a little kudos to the band that rang the bell on my predecessor's plot, but discussing past and future me and a similar you? Well, you'd have to take a sip of my life brew, three parts hard spirit, a heap of point of view, two parts tasty mixer. Now, for just a little dash of you. Shaken, not stirred, that bartender deserves his due, because from right here, a secret agent we'll pursue.

Aye alright, I know, where the fuck does Bond fit with the mirrors in this lengthy rhetoric? Ok, I'll admit, perhaps I wrote this under the influence of vice and fix, but sobriety of mind doesn't change the point. We hunt an enemy, or perhaps a mole inside your organisation, so you'll never dissuade me from this war that I've been waging.

Vampiric Pen

I've eaten food like a fiend and drank myself into bitter fuckin' dreams. Been round shooters, no girls, just Nike tracksuits, Gucci, Supreme. Real dangerous fuckin' men. If not now, then when? Gotta feed this vampiric pen, it's become my only friend, cos where I'm from talking can bring to a man a quick and fateful death, man dem.

I knew a few youths who now reside in the ground cos they peeped to the po; the hitters crept without a sound. The streets be ready to go, the streets be ready to blow. Braat! Braat! Give the mo'fuckin' street king his crown. You'll all bow down. Give man that chain. Give champ that belt. Got so many P's weather man says it's gonna be raining all week.

Talk is cheap, say it with man's chest. If you decide to come at me you better be at your best, cos if you ain't, man won't breathe long enough to worry about any of that regret. Booyah!

Monstrous Machine

The monstrous machine greased and oiled by the crooked regime.
They be printing all that paper; fat cats got all our fuckin' cream.
From the rich to the fiend, and the poor masses in between.
My paycheck is stretched so thin, it's butcher's dog lean.
We've heard it all before, banking crisis, Iraq war.

The cogs that turn the world have razor sharp teeth,
it's fuelled by money and sanctioned by the lord.

Queen and Country

What's it come to when the Queen is almost dead, and the country is on its knees. There are millions out of work with an ample percentage holding degrees. Then another quartile is striking endlessly. Then a number more wade on, through the torrent of hardship. Broke, broken Britain breaking up families.

While the corrupt appallingly applaud, house party at Commons or the House of Lords? That's a sickness for which there's no mandatory vaccine. While the war on drugs still wages on, a new one in the Ukraine has gone and begun. Is clearing the streets as unachievable as ever achieving peace?

The Captain and the Lover

Drinks served on the bar of the Titanic II, remind me
of a time when I loved being with you. A lighthouse
in the morning mist, but more often the smoke, when
I needed saving you were there with the rope.
How many times, my love, can you keep this tub
afloat?
Those lifelines become nooses, and there's holes in the
boat.

Out to sea; the waters churn.
Out to sea; a soul begins to yearn.

All those nautical miles tied me in Gordian knots, but
maintain present course, I want mine neat on the
rocks. You're becoming a drag; you anchor my sad as
I search for scraps of dignity in sealy bags. You told
me I was dashing, then saw the blue lights flashing.
Sparrows are migrating, the Lusitania's tanking.

Out to sea; we fought those storms together.
Out to sea; you always changed like the weather.

Paint me like one of your French girls, Jack, just as the
portrait of Mr. Grey, but make sure the paint doesn't
crack. I promise there's a life raft made for two, shame
you never cared to show me the escape route.

Math's was never my strong suit, nor was I the brains, but it felt like some six times three hundred sixty-five days, give or take, more or less, that and some change.
Remember days when booty wasn't the main aim of the game, love carried its own value, and we weighed it the same?
Now the silver in my pocket only gleams in vain.

Out to sea; you loved the shine of the moon.
Out to sea; my maps, only X leads to you.

So, when I said your name rhymed with malicious intent, there's a stowaway on board, and she demands I repent. Green eyes of the storm always led me astray. It was hard to find my way home when I lived in your name. You always told me to look for my little northern star but your lustre couldn't muster enough light to burn away all my dark.

Out to sea; blood taints the blue.
Out to sea; the shark's orbit, ensues.

Paint me like one of your French girls, Jack, just as the portrait of Mr. Grey, but make sure the paint doesn't crack. With all these Wins let's celebrate with a table for two, in the belly of the beast, and it's me on the menu.

When the inspectors arrive, Sharky and George...
that's childhood nostalgia; It's real blood on the floor.
The cabin saw the violence but couldn't talk anymore,
the victims are all memories and they lay in their
scores. But this isn't a cruise, there ain't no murder
mystery, it's a hulking ghost ship hauling kilotons of
misery.

Out to sea; a captain stays his course.
Out to sea; the mermaids call in your voice.

Another poor captain goes down with the ship, amid
your lunar eclipse. That taste on your lips. I've
drowned so many times in you, I'll give you Davey
Jones' tips. Here's the keys to my locker, uniform's
like brand new. The glory fades on Jaws Themed
Swimming. Besides, you got me feeling real blue.

Out to sea; I shared my treasure with you.
Out to sea; mutinous hearts, stir the crew.

Paint me like one of your French girls, Jack, just as the
portrait of Mr. Grey, but make sure the paint doesn't
crack. Now, as heartbeats quicken on this saltwater
bed, kick off those concrete shoes and let me fuck
with your head.

I found the heart shaped treasure, a Nagasaki hand grenade. One becomes destroyer of worlds, you're one of the greats. Like Oppenheimer's Frankenstein in Anne Summers' lace, my Promethean courtesan, Hyde's better face.
An addiction, my affliction, the course that I'd always take. My true north, always right time, right place. My first class, my first mate but I'd always be late, lose cargo on the way, and when security trumps love, you need faux, and I'm just, fake.

Out to sea; two lovers' business concludes.
Out to sea; I'll make sure the devil, gets his dues.

Found a message in a bottle washed up, like me, on a bar, where Captain Morgan always keeps me a seat and they don't ever charge. Beverly and Mary-Jane, this company that I keep, til' I'm skull and bones, let it be known it's a pirate this heart seeks.

Out to sea; the captain's drunk at the helm.
Out to sea; I'll sail this bitch, straight into hell.

Paint me like one of your French girls, Jack, just as the portrait of Mr. Grey, but make sure the paint doesn't crack. Oh, my darling you took me right to the stars, and for that here's your gift, half a wasted life in Kilner jars.

After a year of marauding and drunken regrets, told many I could be their best worst mistake yet. Cast off the mutiny of crows from around my nest, hauled up my anchor from the fathomless depths. Now my crew has new faces, but all passed the test, perhaps this battle-scarred bucket, has got some life in her yet.

Out to sea; night yields to the dawn's demands.
Out to sea; the horizon gives way to land.

Out to sea; a captain retakes his vessel.
Out to sea; the tempest, is my temple.

A sparrow returns north, and Jack nears his end, this old captain sips the old poison, again. If there's a lesson in this, perhaps it is to whit, don't lose your treasure, 'cos you may never, ever find you again.

World Wor

Many moons have passed but many moons I spent sitting on the edge of our Ardennes Forest bed. Cruel words fall like bombs, vocalised lead, but as a prisoner of this war, you still get your head…Stormin' Norman-dy, lost count of love's casualties, we've taken cupid's bullets and we've drowned in your sea, we've even picked up limbs blown off by artillery. In this film we're saving Private You, naïve that you're the enemy. Kids with guns fired caps and shot blanks, I've made the great escape and I've died on the sand.

Those thin red lines have pumped rouge life through these hands…a pulmonary pummelling performed pre-dawn; pre-emptive heart attacks make this a proxy war. Now D-day's every day, breach team, please blow this door.

So…can you go AWOL on me and you? Left your comrade waiting for his army of two, but twelve years stained our democracy hypoxically blue, Captain Scarlett's the only truth that I knew.

Crimson was my colour, my ancestral claim, but I thought the cloth that wove our fate would cut just the same. Sitrep please, I need medical aid. You always blamed O_2, I'll take the lies all the same. Compressions help the rhythm of the drummer in the rain, but as this heart beats faintly, incarcerated in its cage, the lungs stay disconnected, can't pay this bill with his name.

Your chains in the mail, sorry it's delayed. A prime Amazonian queen takes her place, swings and round tables take us back to that place, when Arthur met that lady at a Northumbrian Lake.

Sorry for the digression from this historical lesson. My lexical blitzkrieg hides metaphoric intention, as spies lacking spines cross battle lines, you know my darling, espionage is out of style. While you were in the wind, I dug a trench made for two. If only I'd known about that hotel room. The name wasn't yours but, my little pseudo-nympho, I won't lose your trail cos I'm hearing Morse code repeating your name, SOS can sound like soz, an ambush waiting in its place. I said you're an enigma and you laughed in your way. Only when in your arms, I knew that I'd lost the race.

Sometimes a woman's touch, however abrupt, if one has the mind to read or listen to a book, you'd understand that as a man, they chart your final course, from mother, lover, sister, aunt, or wife, my word, of course! We die in the name of God and Wor country. Makes sense for most relationships to need a co-signatory.

Til' death do us part, we join in matrimony, conscription proves conviction, and we've always adored ye. So please provide political posterity to Wor monotheistic sanctuary. We needed your approval to know we were meant to be, because we all know government and God are good for me and thee.

Your chain's in the mail, sorry it's delayed. A prime Amazonian queen takes her place, swings and round tables take us back to that place, when Arthur met that lady at a Northumbrian Lake.

Ok, look a knaa, hinny, the Tyne's my only sea, a Geordie lad's colloquial acorn sprouts its tree. Divven't kid yourself ya knaa for a second what I mean. I've barked and bowed up to now, in the tongue of monarchy but strong oaks grow where the northern winds blow, wor kid, I'd never wish to be from London town, or Efowich, the name's Dunholm ya see. On with wor northern legend; me owld Granda spilled the beans…'My boy I've seen them die, think nightmares on Benidorm beach. Seen heroes go to hell and cowards win their wars, al never lie to you, my boy, life gives nee fucking quarter, not for any one of us, my son, my kin, my daughter. Firing squad won't wait for orders.'

Old man leans in close, and he takes a breath, line baited in the water, and we both bite with the best. Your grandma raised a gentleman, hold the door and dress your best. Or Grandad raised a lady, all manners and respect.

Your chain's in the mail, sorry it's delayed. A prime Amazonian queen takes her place, swings and round tables take us back to that place, when Arthur met that lady at a Northumbrian Lake.

So, if it's Tyne or the Wear, or it's Tee's time in here, we started in bed, soft words in the ear. I whispered I love you, voice heavy with fear, but I promise you wor lass, you'll never see any tears. Wor lad, don't kid yourself, I'm not fresh down with this rain, we're a triple entente playing a two-player game.

VietDan

I'm crazy like the glue but my bonds don't always stick. Adhesion needs cohesion and I'm a bit of a dick, but you won't ever need to clean up my drunken sick or worry about the burn time on the little man's wick. I know you've been mistreated, misfit. I been punked like you but if dead Kennedys can present to me, a picture of the world most never even see, I can see me in you.

Reet, so history comes hand in hand with me, learned it all young, inquisitively, but 'boring' ain't an adjective that jives with this human bean, cos you can't get to where you're going if you don't know where you've been.

Know you might wanna wash your hands when handling me cos I eat gutter sharks, well after dark, plenty carrots help me see. Those old wives' tales put wind in your sails, but ya mammy won't be the guide to your holy grail, and she sure won't make you me. I learned this shit in VietDan, the war of the nineties, and noughties, no matter what you ever bought me. The cost of war is high when sons get spent overseas, a comparable parable a millennial can't be.

So, fuck you, government, police and policy, a human can't ever perpetrate the crime of slavery. With 20/20 vision, a corona round our sun, we condemn, taste the steel of our gun, be it Davey Smith or Gillian Wesson, been centuries since your class learned a lesson. Class to me used to be, years one through six, then seven to eleven, but my sister, that was just a trick, iller than the illest illusion you ever witnessed, doubt cast in the courtroom, jury stacked with convicts.

'Convicts of what?' you ask. We're your fucking peers! You couldn't peer into my soul in a hundred-million years! That's a billion if you're asking, the price tag of your fear, I see you at the livestock ranch, selling all your gear. You're a real-deal cardboard farmer, passive-aggressive intent, real motherfuckers live the life you sell to pay your lass for the rent.

Let's face it, embrace it, ain't like you had a real one in a while, cuddle in super close, grant yourself a smile. The other side of this box-sprung warzone, dogs bark at a razor fence and the prisoner inside you sees a minefield called resentment. I'm critical, and cynical, I see that you can easily forget. In this story I'm the Attenborough, you're just my subject.

Perhaps you're photogenic but my voice is really smooth. Heard that wisdom's experienced but knowledge is learned, you fool. Don't have to fly to see why my wisdom ledger's canny full, and you know, less than a ledge has no room for dancing shoes.

Now those dad jokes are set aside watch how a real man makes his move. You're a mirage in the desert, while I've got nothing left to prove.

Claimed a stake on this gold, and got one for your heart, if I interviewed a vampire, wow...you'd get the part. On Le Stadt de Roullion, you said you loved art, but lecherous intentions, they drove us apart. As much as I loved a night out you were always my worst part. Don't start, this race is over before I forgot it had begun, we got garlic by the clove and loaded, venomous puns.

From dusk in your musk, to dawn when I'm torn, see the light of a new day cast on a lovely summer morn, but when I take a step into that green hued dew, it's like we were born again anew. Sometimes it takes fire to blaze trails in new directions, don't worry if it's treacherous, I've got magnetic intentions, and if polar-opposites attract, you've got my attention. You're the Santy to my claws, promised I'd leave a first impression.

Foil, Toil, Trouble on the Boil

Sometimes a soul may escape through a hole, a decimal point sized space in the mould. Growth was inspired and like water I flowed, until nowt was left of me, flames turn to turned over coals in the snow. You treat me like dirt, but my ambitions more soil, I'm growing hardier harvests these days. Salted land takes hard toil. If your cauldron bubbles then mine's on the boil. I see the witching hour more than most, and the worry of which witch could cause the most trouble.

Coveted covens conveniently convene with cacophonous sounds crashing through the trees, smoked a few of those and wor kid I can see, a death knoll is just a bell, reminding you to believe. Leave all your grudges, dead leaves make way for seeds. Life casts enough shade, don't create your own canopy.

So, forget hocus-pocus. You poke holes in my focus, all I needed was a point perhaps you could be my locus. Points can be weapons like rapier meets foil or dropped like ordinance on your life's civilians. Suppose every blade still needs its oil. My point is, if on witch hunts our history is hidden or rewritten, that's a Faustian bargain if ever I heard one, many clamour to be that goat. We're the greatest of all time, yet ever more divided and remote. We used to use words to build bridges, they weren't always over moats.

Transport is a Pain

Times are for trains and I'm off the tracks, late to the station. God, I was beaten black. I railed against the feeling, at the thought of paying that fine. But I could never ignore that northern line, calling me right back.

If you've got a ticket to ride, let's take a trip together. Through fairy tales, through the veil, forget about the weather. I'll show you a world that glitters like pearls, two birds of an iridescent feather. So, whether a flock or a murder, I'll put the crow in your crown and wait on your platform forever.

Times are for flights, and I'm bored of hearing final calls. Pilot lights out again, Wish I could warm your daughters' halls. This plane of existence only holds the colours of my regret. We've winged this whole relationship. Oh, let fly, impoverished laments.

If you've got a ticket to ride, let's take a trip together. Through fairy tales, through the veil, forget about the weather. I'll show you a world that glitters like pearls, two birds of an iridescent feather. So, whether a flock or a murder, I'll put the crow in your crown and wait on your platform forever.

Times owned by pain. I booked us passage on a ship. It's got a lot of lifeboats to save you drowning in one liners. I've been cruising for a bruising, tired of being a single diner. Though this cabin was for us, it seems it's just full of loss, and a constant, cloying reminder.

If you've got a ticket to ride, let's take a trip together. Through fairy tales, through the veil, forget about the weather. I'll show you a world that glitters like pearls, two birds of an iridescent feather. So, whether a flock or a murder, I'll put the crow in your crown and wait on your platform forever.

On Hold

Hold the line for your life, hold the line for your money, been on hold so fuckin' long that it has ceased being funny. Thirty minutes, thirty hours, thirty months, thirty days. Thirty plus years ain't seen too much go my way. Does this mean I should approach every day with such rampant distress? Like a hungover honey bear all claws and bad breath?

I need relief from the night times alone in my bed. Carnival's in full swing in my head, because of what? A distinct lack of ched? Please man, we're starving. All we need is some bread. I'm sorry peeps, yeah, forget it. All the dough, yeah, they ate it. It's hard to swallow like a bitter pill, don't you just hate it? Work a full-time job, still always stuck on E credit. Overdrawn, overspent. Does the snapping jaw and hunger of life never relent?

If I believed in a god and I wasn't so spent; forgiveness, please Allfather I truly repent. On hold for half an hour, another cold shower, gas gets cut off just like my calls drop, I'm powerless to restore power. *Suppose the screams* from below from seeds sown amongst your impoverished sisters, brothers and others.

No one heeds, individual needs.

We all *just make up the sounds* of the machine and right now it seems they've got it running sweet.

Intermission

Made it this far, have you? Fair play. I sit here late on a Friday night, thinking of you. The faceless, discerning reader. How does my writing make you feel? Can you relate? Do you find some comfort or does it shock and disgust you. I'd be happy with any of that list, means I'm provoking/evoking emotions.

Stories from the streets can't ever be clean. That would be like expecting to find an honest politician or a recreational crackhead. It is what it is. When you get caught in the trap of believing that everything else is to blame for your own actions and constant need for whatever it is that fuels you, that is a real tough spot.

If you choose to give up parts of yourself to things, ensure the things have some value or nourishment for who you are or what you wish to become. Make them transactional in a positive way. Don't waste time doing shit that makes you worse.

Even if it feels good, perhaps especially so.

Addiction for me has been a battle. I'm sure you can see with the imagery, that I've felt somewhat under the cosh! But I've had plenty of time to consider things.

I was at war with myself.

Mobb Deep said it best 'Ain't no such things as halfway crooks.'

That's exactly what I was becoming. I was all the way in, once upon a time. But that was when I was young, damaged and ignorant. These next pieces reflect the change. One foot in, one foot out. Didn't know if I'd make it.

I didn't learn any of this overnight. It took me years to cultivate the perfect storm of fuck-ups before I finally tried something different. You're always learning on the job, with life. The seven-day weeks can become exhausting, and I used to reward myself heavily for barely scraping by, unsteady in both work and stride. Sick note Steve. But I was sick, sick of the cycle of debt and depression and anxiety and drugs and alcohol.

Of course they were all linked, but when the vicious cycle spins up like a circular saw, it feels a lot more dangerous trying to stop it with your own bare hands. But that's what I'm here trying to do, I've nearly lost a limb once due to my own desperation. At least this one would be worth it. The consumption has ceased and it's now the time for a stage of metamorphosis.

PART II –
THE CHRYSALIS

"I think that he would rather suffer anything than entertain these false notions and live in this miserable manner."

Plato, The Republic, Allegory of the cave

"Sometimes we motivate ourselves by thinking of what we want to become. Sometimes we motivate ourselves by thinking about who we don't ever want to be again."

Shane Niemeyer

"One of the hardest things was learning that I was worth recovery."

Demi Lovato

Seven-Thirty

It was seven thirty on a night in ninety-six, or twenty twelve, or any date you could think. Some poor family's lost a brother, lost a father, lost a son. Through illness and accident, bullet and gun. With malicious intent, death's silent song. So, toll the bell, little boy blue, there are monsters at the door, and they're here for you.

Little man lost, never to be found. No rhyme or reason, so when chaos abounds, crank out that song, and be sure to sing loud, because one day we'll all be singing from the ground.

As the cold wind buffets thick white snow, the door at your back squeaks on the floor. You're shaking like leaves when winter gales blow. Those monsters can smell you, feel your pulse grow, as it beats out a quickening tattoo. Wood splinters, then cracks, sharp claws meet your back.

Little man lost, never to be found. No rhyme or reason, logic or sound. rank out that song, and be sure to sing loud, because one day we'll all be singing from the ground.

Anyone who's lived through the hurt known from loss, knows a new meaning to that little word 'cost'. Each little cut is a tick on your bill, doesn't take long for your ticker to fill. I know mine's mainly scars, a bit of tape and glue, an ounce of ambition, and the flame of hope too. Not hope for me, but I guess hope for you, because those monsters are dangerous, kill one, make two.

You feel the ribbons, torn from your skin, those lies you told, are taking chunks out of the man you could be. You're never ever too smart not to get caught, you feel the bite of guilt, teeth clamp down, and test out your lungs. That breathless feeling starts to mix with the blood, the blood you spilled by cups, of all the ones that you've ever loved. Pain wracks your body, you're begging to be nailed back up, cos martyrdom seems like the ultimate repayment, but saying sorry and being honest are always, just enough.

Let's get your body mended, stitched and all fixed up, the monsters left you to be food, for the dogs. They left you for good, they left their marks on you, but boy, my boy you're standing back up. The sun breaks through the blinds and warms you in the glow of its touch, look to the door and see it's been hung back up and put together like a jigsaw, just finished with an artisanal touch. Head to it, reach out a steady hand and open it up, you found yourself my boy, now get out there and re learn to run.

Little boy lost; little man found. No monsters in sight and good weather abounds. All together now, crank out that song, and be sure to sing loud, every single day that we can, with our chorus from the ground.

Demons

Father please I beg of you, exorcise these demons. They've lived inside me for so long, all I feel is dread and darkness. They've become my friends;

protectors...

and when you tear them from my body...

will it feel like a slight, pinch or will the pain be roaring and relentless. When I listen, I can hear them speaking, hatching plans and slowly teaching. Laughter in the deep, claws and talons reaching, pulling me down, to where I exist beneath them.

They have taken control, and they keep me imprisoned. My cell has one window with which I am allowed to witness them. They tear up the pieces of my life I love the most; taunt me with their treason; they relish showing me the rope. A noose for a neck that needed winding in. A gun to the head of a life that was deemed nearly ruined. A slug to the chest that was always profanely shouting. Poison for the stomach that was always doubting. Pokers for the eyes that saw nothing but disgrace. Sandpaper used to rub away a liar's pretty face.

So, left in this cell to my rot and to my fervour. Feverish tremors rack this physical form I've come to name nobody. Call them *No* for short because it's the only word he knows. *No* chance of retribution, *no* to walks through pristine snow. *No* to the idea of forgiving, *no* to believing, *no* to living, *no* to help, *no* to hands that wish to hold, *no* to even continued breathing.

These demons are my jailer, and they hold the secret and the key. They feast on scraps of skin and sinew that nobody called me. They've fed on the goodness and the light fantastic.

Consumed all I knew, all I am, all I had been. They rattle on my door, as I rattle in my chains. Father, can you save us, or is salvation just *pretend?*

Digging Bones

I've known downs and I've known pick-me-ups; now when I'm down, I know you'll pick me up. When you're around I get that Midas touch, as diamonds go, you're flawless, I'm one in the rough.

Like an archaeologist excavating old *bones*, I carefully dust away time's trauma, sediment and stone. We were found to tessellate, like corresponding shapes, I was just in time, not to be too late. Got stoned with a bone, that really felt like my home, in carbon I asked for a date.

You got history my darling, I do too, but it's my favourite subject, let me be an expert in you. Our favourite colour is green, you chased away the blues, made my sun shine in rainbow prism hues. In bleak, black nightmares, like prey we were pursued. Please, take my hand, we must slip into our predatory shoes.

Too long we've been starving for feelings with nutritious value. I know I've got the oats, and grains of my sand timer have finally hit mature. So, my lady, if I dare, while I'm feeling so sure and true, you gave me this sword I write with, may I pledge it to you?

I'm bewitched and I'd battle a thousand bastards just to be with you. At the start of things, an end is created. Fear and uncertainty crash all around us, unabated, but with a wry little smile and a wink of an eye that shines like a sapphire, all those hungers you have sated. I'll always be your blood diamond, trialled in combat, made under pressure, prophetically fated.

I had a wound the depth of a lagoon, tears filled it up and it was surrounded by dunes. Robbed 'em all be it, Peter or Paul, yet you spiced up my life and I heeded your call. Horns sounded from Gondor, could the North truly fall? They've come for my *bones* and they're breaching the walls. I'd be the fastest Rohan rider to be thrown into the fold, show you true sacrifice, shelter you from cold. Hold you in the night when terrors march out of the snow, for you I'd climb a mountain yet with life, I can barely cope. It's champion, I was your champion, the viper claims another face.

I see reanimation in those old *bones*, a life seeking confidence and worth, better still, little phoenix, you'll claim glory and rebirth, for I'm a willing disciple at your church, thy will be done, through all the love and the hurt.

I'll come to an end like this and hope the meaning hits. I've spent years in the hurt chewing the dirt, grit and glass chipped away at broken teeth. Two black eyes, bruised and battered, burst lips utter a cry. With righteous indignation, I fire from the hip. I had been shooting blanks, you made me a tank, you're an oasis to this desert rat. I was too focused on the bread and butter to see that your cheddar didn't come in a trap.

With care, passion and love, that fits like a glove, perhaps a mouse can befriend a cat. But I feel a lot more staffy, all loyal smiles and happy, like you rescued me from Battersea, gave your time willingly, to see the real me. So, thank you for fulfilling one of my life's dreams, to know a love as vast as the universe, burning with every star I can see.

Bird Vs. Person

This is a recitation by a national treasure. Feel like my mood's always dressed for inclement weather. Maybe it comes from being British. Could it come from being poor? Seems it comes from not giving two fucks anymore. Down on your luck, dying to break that duck? Then I'm with you right there, we're birds of a feather.

My plumage ain't the cleanest though I've never built a sturdy nest yet. But my beauty comes from this heart-shaped patch nature blessed upon this chest. So, I puff it out proud and like the songbird I am…and begin to sing. It's the summer outside, not a cloud in the sky. Time I soared out, no more clipped wings. Flying makes it easy to get sky high.

Sorry, back to being miserable, drown yourself in wailing woe. Allow yourself to be so glum you're not just a lead balloon, you're a hundred fucking ton. Break your neck to check on the misery, keen to loan some when none's found. I have an active bitch face at all times, frowning keeps people out of bounds.

Bounds to be heading south for the winter, warm up this icy beak. Look for a mate for life, done just mating for the night. Taking flight that way just ain't for me. I mean, as a bird I must fly, but rarely will I flee. I've learned from the shame now I follow the wind, currents guiding to where I must be. *C'est la vie.*

Alright, enough with all this tweety bird bullshit. It's stupid in the Nth degree. The only thing on the agenda today is self-serving, self- loathing and agony. You know life's gonna kick you, then kick you again. Spit in your face then pretend to be a friend. Then sneak into your bed in the middle of the night. Push you back down and steal your bike. So, heed what I say, better to befriend, a benevolent dismay, easier to expect disappointment, from you or others that way.

Back from the winter sun, let's gather the materials for my home. I've built in high in a rookery this time, plenty bedding and shelter for my 'tweety bird' family. See, what that miserable miser doesn't know is, while his heart's frozen, ice under heavy snow, mine flies high for all to see. So, when you're feeling like that guy, remember you, too, can fly. Remember you've got heart, little bird, and you're *enough for me.*

For the Bairns

Another father tells lies and two little girls cry, it was never his aim, but they've been made to feel the blame of that letter from their mother's solicitor. That will live with those lasses no matter how much time passes. Their inner children always feel that hurt. So, when they're mistreated, abused by the rest, bet they wish you could feel it all.

Little boy blue in the corner, many behavioural disorders. Thrown to familial predators, like a lamb to the slaughter. Given the choice between loss of innocence and never feeling anything at all. Looking deep into those broken blue grey eyes, see all the horrors that lie behind. He whispers, barely audible, like one breath into open air. Words that linger. Those words… "tough call."

Two twins hold hands while crossing the road from their bullies, making haste to the safety of bedrooms and plushies. Past ghosts of parents, be they the workers or the drunks. Up to their sanctum, safe and remote. Then the vibrations begin, screens fill up with words compelling suicide, phones ring. Videos and insults hurled through the internet of things. No one asked, nor did anyone seem to acknowledge their plight, so they both took their own lives, holding each other tight. Two parents find their bodies, two more broken people, feeling appalled.

Pay attention to our youth, young ones, bairns, the children. We owe it to the kids we were to be better, not indifferent. Encourage open dialogue, ask the hard questions. Teach the hard lessons, tell them all your best ones. Remember they're akin to you, only you know how you were raised. Could you honestly say, with a hand on your heart, you'd have it done exactly the same? Does the good outweigh the bad in yours? Or are you only teaching what you project:

Fear.

Guilt.

Blame.

Packing up Promises

Sitting surrounded by a life that could truly have been yours, but is that the truth or just a point of view? Swear I'm always closing doors. Could this be purgatory? I'm sure they saw me, calling for help, begging reprieve? Perhaps they only saw a beast, stalking between the trees.

These ornamental boxes, full of someone else's memories, I've none of my own, at least not physically. Spent so long living in my past, most thought I'd never come back but when you hear voices you missed, on the wind through the mist, it's hard not to follow the breeze.

Sweeping up the dirt of hollow little words, never meant a single one of them, but I'd swear I meant them all. If you truly meant it, you say, there'd not be bags packed in the hall. Been high for way too long my son, you were due a tragic fall.

How can you
         fall

 further

than the bottom?

Again, it's a viewpoint, a lack of understanding.

You've hit eject without your parachute; you might not survive this landing. What you thought was your lowest, was merely below us. Your negligent naiveté makes this hole bottomless.

But what's that?

A

single

rope,

the most *malnourished* strand of hope? How can one carry a fallen comrade when you have wounds with which you cannot cope? How can one hope to ever be more than just a single unit, never knowing what it feels like, when two ones become two?

So, with mud on his face, clothes splattered with disgrace, he approaches these new days with a smile on his face. Not the face he shows the world but the face that he holds inside; a face that lives and loves and trusts, fed a daily dose of pride. A lion heart roars out of the dark, he knows he can stand out in the crowd, cleaned up his face, cleaned up his act, did things he had never really tried.

How's the story end? It's a beginning again. The author's got sober, he's putting in the work, some murderous thrillers, some mysteries, some real tear-jerkers, pages soaked with loss and love, his own version of a happily ever after. When a person suffers a lifetime's worth of calamity yet is still left with redemption outweighing the insanity...sure, he can move this saga along at a pace, replace mistakes with positivity.

The author always felt like someone else, I never truly knew him as me.

The Dog Knight

Hard to be a hero when filled with malicious intent.
He's crazy! Yeah maybe. The pressure builds with my dissent.
Behave properly? Yeah, stop me. It's self-destruction I represent.
Broken bones and broken promises, a boozed-up bulldog blows a vent. Then a gasket, grave dug casket.
But that's a bottle with no bottom?
Yeah, that's just how he asked for it.
Would rather drink himself to death than ever *bury the fucking hatchet.*
Drunk as the proverbial skunk, forever black and white.
Same colours as a priest, but he's closer in spirits to Benedictine, than monk.
Thought you said he was a dog?
Yeah, he's been a real street living hound. Bit more than one family that took him in from the pound.
If the dog bites, should it really be put down?
Or should we *stop and think*…What created the desperation that gave way to snarls and gnashing teeth?
This aloof pooch got a roof, love and food but fluid intake of a fish.
But he shuns it all for the liquids howling call, made all those dog's dinners into a real feast.
North of the border, there's some social disorder. Voicemail recorder, this court demands we have order.

Your actions are contemptible, and you will be charged as such.
You're a danger to those around you.
A degenerate flippant, plonky punk.
Now, remove yourself from this courtroom and stop wasting our time. No need to adjourn.
Have a prison term, no less than six long lonely months.
So, now the dogs gone to court?
Yeah, the court of public opinion;
a unanimous conviction, the true cost was his predilection.
He'd been lost for a time, between vineyard and vine.
Playing homemade hopscotch on hand drawn lines.
When your whole life has been survival your honour, it's easy to lose sight of your crimes.
Think I get it now. The dog's a metaphor, for the man it represents?

If you're with me this far, oblige me by staying until the end.
An animal from the ends, eats from the gutter, eats his friends, eats his family, eats himself, again and again.
Now he's a lonesome puppy, crying for Mummy, crying for money, crying for her, crying when?
Crying tears of ink from his broken pen.
So, how fairs our hero?
Has he begun to make amends?
Yeah, he's sober, near October, little crosses begin showing bigger trends.
Working hard becoming legit, too much graft quitting to ever quit.
He says the mental clarity is quite sublime.

Quietly he will do his time, recovery the only remit.
So, he's fixed?
Nah, not even close.
However, the story has a new hope, and every day not on it is a step back from gibbet and rope.

His chivalric virtues were always there.
But in armour as dull as his stare, sword that's blunted from duelling with life. From dawn's break, to moonlight, a poorly maintained person's passing for a fairy tale knight.
But when he returned from battle...
Yeah?
He slept in his helmet every night.
Never let anyone close, his excuses verbose, changed was the man from facing plight after plight.
Riddled with doubt was he, how does he stop his fated regression?
Yeah, I'm getting to that. An excellent question.
The answer, however, was simple:

He just had to **learn his lesson.**

Taught himself to love himself, to reconcile the pain, to pay more attention.
Mean the words, stick to every date.
It'll take all his might to resist the urge to alight.
Free from the duty he swore in their names.
I'll leave it here for the day but please don't dismay!
We're only halfway through the flight, and we know our boy ain't scared of the fight.

My prediction? Decision win, mark those calendars for February.

Queens to me

Even with no strings attached, I'm your marionette. When the heads start to roll, you're my Marie Antoinette. My queen please meet old lady guillotine, all those livres for your life. The people demand a price, this love demands a sacrifice.

Accused of adultery like Anne Boleyn, when I've got an axe to grind, mind mired in malicious sin. My queen, please meet old man haft and blade. Best laid plans and promises made, but above the dark water of the Thames, you await, like Jane Grey, unfulfilled and afraid.

Seeking out my Jezebel. My Phoenician lady lives by the sea where hearts swell. My queen, please meet old lady ledge, falling, flailing in your finery. As you are Jezebel, and he is Elijah. You dared to be equal in the times of the patriarchal tyrants. Perhaps that hasn't changed.

So, marry me in the eyes of a god. Who cast your kind asunder, left to misogynistic plunder. My queen, please meet old man religion. Perpetrator and practitioner of sky daddy's power. Though dynamics change, and when I say your name: it is Hatshepsut by decree.

A *queen* treat as divinity.

A *goddess* given life again.

A *goddess* only known only to me.

Tightrope

Ever felt like walking on a tightrope, trying to stay balanced? One slip of the wrong words from your lips leads to arguments then parlance. Carrying the weight of the world on this back, do I really have a chance? Or was the fall always coming under a clear sky where stars dance?

Lonely it is treading along this thread, look to one side and the other, see your imminent demise between towering structures. Alone, suspended above it all hearing echoes of loved ones below, who call, with words of encouragement, praise and support. This could be the hardest round I've ever fought. Can I maintain this razor focus while praying the wire beneath faltering feet remains taut?

Left foot, right foot. One leads the other. Either keep toeing this line or fall back into the gutters. The wire stretches off into the distance and I can see no end. My stride is sure to falter and my words sure to offend. I can never explain myself because to know me you'd need a map, to navigate the pitfalls, tripwires and traps.

Onwards I must go until I reach some kind of conclusion. I'm so tired I'm seeing double, ghoulish illusions whose allusions, lead me back to those times of responsibility's diffusion. Taunted by the tightrope and hallucinating my past. The first slip leads my tiny audience to gasp.

Falling, clutching for a saviour, don't wish to overuse a cliché trope. Hanging on by bloody fingertips to fibres made to choke my hope. I'm back walking again on the hangman's rope. Trying to climb that slipperiest of slopes. Falling seems like freedom but there's no way I'd recover, no way I would cope.

Trudge on, lonely soldier, you can make it back home. Keep pushing yourself forward down this tightrope of forever. Just trying to be better that's my only endeavour. This is why I keep putting one foot in front of the other.

Suits You

Spent too long wrapped up in the past like Alice staring into the looking glass. I fell into a dream and became lost to our world like I was living in the third person. Watching me, watching it all. It certainly became all about the money, it was the finest car crash TV. Before it all got real I could see the appeal. Looking back now it stole more than it ever healed.

Felt like I had ceased to be real –
like a ghost can pass through solid objects. I was passing through my life and that of others. I was a phantom acting out a play. Ever felt that? Someone close in an empty room. Like someone stepped over your grave. That little shudder is what I became.

The notoriety was too much fame. Never had a taste for it really. But it became the costume worn out in the world. Phone calls with *whens* and *wheres.* Making paper disappear. But when that magic runs out and your mask keeps on slipping, the face beneath reveals the fear.

Scared of hanging up my identity, the person I'd been for eight hundred and thirty-two weeks. Most of my time, could it be a life term? How many zigs do I have left before I zag into oblivion? Can you afford to relinquish the tried and tested method that owns you
–

to make something of your own?

For now, I'm back from the dream and I only see myself in the mirror. I'm back from the dead and I'm feeling pretty chipper. Bit like Prince charming just turned up with my glass slipper. Feels like I'm wearing myself again, only this time my tailor's way better.

Intermission Two

If the road to hell is paved with good intention, then what is the road to recovery paved with? So far, it's been hard work, quiet evenings and a seductive song that whispers you back into the bottle you've managed to escape from. I won't be trapped in there again like a tiny ship's captain. But it is, every day, a choice I make to ignore the siren song until it ceases its baleful beckoning.

Some would say I have been a man of substance for some time. More like substances. I'm hoping that I am emerging as something new, something better without them. It hasn't been a straight course.

I've been considering love and its impact on me for some time. As you've read, I have words for much love and heartbreak. It is a double-edged sword. It is the purest form of joy to love and be loved. To share laughter on a summer's day. An embrace on a cosy night in. That warmth and pressure holding you tight in the wee hours. But to love someone truly is to allow yourself to become vulnerable. To put someone else before yourself; to expose who you are and what makes you tick; to rely they will be there when you need them; to trust in blind faith, even if every other event in your life tells you otherwise. Accepting that, with love, inevitably, comes the prospect of loss. This is another lesson I'm learning. Faith isn't something I've had much joy with.

I had to learn to trust again. Trust in myself to be able to do the things I needed to change my life before someone else could. To manage my addictions and clear away the rubble from all the destructive behaviours. Learn to trust the people I choose to involve in my life, not those with which I was forced to be around. I couldn't be trusted myself until I learned this lesson, and the people who know me understand this.

So, like Mama Roux says, "If you don't love yourself; how in the hell you gonna love somebody else?"

I've got me and I've got mine. Found my wings for the second time…

Flap

      flap

  boy

        butterfly…

*PART III –
THE BUTTERFLY*

"With true friends... even water drunk together is sweet enough."
Chinese Proverb

"Every worthy act is difficult. Ascent is always difficult. Descent is easy and often slippery."
Mahatma Gandhi

"Ridiculous for a human being to take 16 years to say, 'I need help.'"
Sir Elton John

Fables From the Storm

I thought that storms were caused by static. Atmospheric passions bring the rain. Tears come unbidden spilling down Mother Gaia's face. What began as a mumble, became a reluctant grumble. Now it's a thunderous rumble setting a chaotic percussive pace.

As the wind section salutes, pipes singing such a sweet rebuke. Even a gentle breeze multiplied by a factor of fifty, could split wood and bend boughs. A hurricane now whips through beleaguered reeds.

Someone's pulling the strings, we're in the kingdom of seven rings, surrounded by Mordor's fires, this all-seeing eye burns like a baleful pyre. A calm and solemn eulogy for the fallen, stranded outside of the wires.

Before all that comes the conductor's light, that conducive flash dictating their orchestral might. Controlling synaptic connections, painted sound into a dark, stormy night. This could be an ode to the endless. Nature's beautiful parting notes.

But when applied to our neurologic map, crocheting complex communicating threads. As the storm begins to wane it leaves in its wake, inside us all a generational memory of fabled stories.

Storm chaser, see you later. Been a tornado for days, whole families hiding in the basement. As you huff and you puff, shaking our little buildings. As a wolf I suppose, pig hating is pure instinct, and this predator comes dressed in lived-in wool.

But it took time, patience, care to darn in knowledge to the ware. Stitched up tears with experience for heavy scars crisscrossed this garment from forgotten hunter's snares. Bullet holes from crack shots, even got attacked in my own lair.

Can a lone wolf ever be guilty of wondering if he can change his murderous hair?

Battlefield

Battlefields of history lay scattered with our dead, dreamers and thinkers with ideas unsaid. Warriors and fighters, cries in their lungs. Brave loving mothers, children clung to the teat, dreaming of embraces, to last through the ages While flames consume lineage, the fire laps at our feet.

Finite though we are, lest we forget. Those who strode before us, knowledge behest, even those without family can wear the bastard's crest.

Infinite though we feel, we travel through tests, death comes to us all, the worst, and the best. The trick to it is to whip up a dish, not let our life make a meal of us.

Two hearts intertwine. Two lovers connect, the laughter may be fleeting, but some feelings accrue interest. Worn by the vicious sand scratch of grief, dashed on the rocks of heartbreak reef, weathered by the loss of your moon and your sun, our fault lines are as frail, as the footsteps of a ghost, in the sand of time, on infinity coast.

Finite though we are, lest we forget. Those who strode before us, knowledge behest, even those without family can wear the bastard's crest.

Infinite though we feel, we travel through tests, death comes to us all, the worst and the best. The trick to it is to whip up a dish, not let our life make a meal of us.

The reason we feel is the reason some steal, some take a life, and others choose to heal. Pieces of puzzles, points on a graph, of an unknown quantification of present, future, past. That's fine with me. The final degree. A fragment of a memory. The root of a tree. But I know I could be your last first, charmingly broken, stuck together with hurt, but more fun to play with. I'll please you with the application of a furtive and respectful, dangerously flirtatious, toy with a story. You'll never tire of these pages.

They say that's the most important part, right... I'll hold you tight and fight all the beasts of heartbreak in the night, been told once, been told twice, but I'm a fool, and I'll court my own plight.

Finite though we are, lest we forget, those who strode before us, knowledge behest, even those without family can wear the bastard's crest.

Infinite though we feel, we travel through tests, death comes to us all, the worst and the best. The trick to it is to whip up a dish, not let our life make a meal of us.

Can't tell you how it's gonna be, can only tell you how it was. What became, what was learned and what was not. Never presume to change the person, just presume to remove doubt.

Let me show you how it is to feel like the only face in a crowd, like a cloud that you can sit on, that's never letting you down.

Thirteen Miles

When did this crown become my iron mask? I've bled before I've passed the flask. Tramped through fields, no meals, pocket full of deals. Thirteen miles I walked, soaked and shod in my eternally shameful past. Blisters that festered in waterlogged boots, those meadows of the mind filled with death and decay, so much carnage, so many bodies, I can feel the dismay.

A stark reminder of my task.

Because edging this *visual insaniam* stands a faceless crowd. They shake their heads and mutter, *verbatim*, the words I've said aloud. Words with which others ran afoul, words hurled, ballistic missiles inbound. Words spat like curses, vainly villainous verses; words, wet with tears, pitter-patter all around. Words tied like notes to cupid's arrow, words filled with love, flittering like spring's sparrow. So many words...they lose all their worth, just wavelengths of sound.

When did this crown become a millstone for the neck, strung out to dry, delightfully dripping wet? But drowning, head pounding, heart rate sounding like a machine gun battle, daylight bombings in my chest. Blistered and festered in burnt and battered boots, in war torn streets identical children play amidst destruction, amidst detritus. Will they ever find their way? Or become victims like all the rest?

Vivamus, moriendum est: Crossing lines doesn't mean you're passing tests.

Because actions speak loudly brazen new intent, actions show vigour, valorous vindication. Actions show you no longer deserve to be in prison. Actions that affect the atmosphere, allow your heaven to burst through those storm laden clouds.

Acta, non verba, hic et nunc.

Forever?

For now.

Small Gods. Big Problems.

Had naught, so give me crosses.

Washed up like flotsam, the sea just tosses me at life's beach. I wonder if it remembers all the other lost souls who reached its' shore. Know before me many came before. Sure, they had their issues, broke some laws. We've all laid washed up while the sea bird's caw.

Dried off in the sun, let it warm my face. Checked for any broken bones, found them all in place. Tattered rags I cast off, even the shawl made of hate. Perhaps I'll make it out alive if I keep going at this rate. Time to stride off this sand so much lighter than I was. Time to ask the hard questions of my pantheon of Gods.

They are many in number and fickle in the extreme. But the undeniable truth is apparent for them all to see. Smiling wide as the cat who got the gold top cream.

"Who comes before us? Who dares to dream? You're not worthy of this heaven; you can't be trusted; You're obscene."

"Don't tell me who I am and I am not, you only exist because of me! This beautiful vista that serves as your home, I grew your knowledge tree."

The gods looked around aghast, seeking support from their peers. I stroll intently among them all growing taller, I strike one down. I see their fear.

"You know now I'm sincere. You may sit and mutter and leer, however I relied on you all to answer my prayers and kick these devils out of here. Just think back to when we were kids. You may feel ageless, but really think. What did we learn when I believed in you all? I really felt you all exist."

"You arrogant upstart, we are timeless. We are dream. We are passion. We are courage. We are muse. We are the eternal unseen. Your question we all will answer as one although you have not asked it. We will show you we allow you to breathe."

I felt the constriction. Echoes of addiction and sadness, bereft. Felt the shawl crawl back around my shoulders. Felt emptied out, with nothing left.

"You wish to know: can you kick this? Survive your affliction? Listen now and listen up. You'll never be free of the food which you need because that which you need needs us."

Needs must.

"We once made a bargain and signed a contract, threw a party, had a blast. Your promises, my Gods, by God's, my god, were they vast! Yet you encouraged my demise and left me hopeless at the last! You grew gluttonous and greedy feasting on relapse after relapse. Eating 's cheating, don't you know. Fat as butter. Time to fast."

They speak in on voice, resonating around their kingdom, walls tremble with vibrations, but I know they'll never fall. I spent the time on strong foundations, used many courses of stone and master masons of course.

"You answered no question, you're a mortal. We are Gods. We rule everything you see and everything that was. We own your heart and your soul, though you promised them to another. We can extinguish your love. We will make you cower! Your insolence and indolence to life they were our nourishment and believe us we will feed. Now, spit out your question, you've always lacked intention, sounded, and without means."

As they stare on in their masses, all raise their glasses. They propose a toast to my defeat. But the clink of the glass, sounded hollow at last. So, there is a bottom, I see.

"Here's the answer to your question..."

They look shocked and bemused;

"I won't ever succumb again to having no food while selling food. Will never again fill your glass, you wretched brood. We learned that the devil's greatest trick, was making me believe he didn't exist. But here you stand in many numbers. Hoping to tear this poor little boy asunder. But I'm wise to your ploy…"

They shrug as one. In fury and years of hellfire boiling Vitruvian: I plough on;

"Oh, don't be so coy. You're the babes of a union between myself and oblivion. Well, time for a fucking family reunion."

Thus begins the slaughter. I take pride in the bloody work. Back breaking *labour* be my saviour, I will serve a righteous cause.

They all scream as one as I devour them, I devour my misbehaviour.

Turns out demon meat, grilled up with some taters, still tastes pretty good when your sober, eight months later.

It's All Getting a Bit Tense

Loss. *Lost*. Lost the plot. Lost the lot. Lost it all. Lost my calling. Lost my family. Lost my father. Lost and the loss just keeps getting harder. Lost waiting to be found. Lost because loss truly has a steep cost.

Find. *Found*. Found a purpose. Found my life. Found a path to follow out of the night. Found fond friends. Found real love. Found the words and picked up my pen. Find I've found more reasons to live, only thing I'm losing these days are the fucks I could give.

Had. Have. Have a reason to be. Have a reason for me. Had so much chaos afoot it was hard to really see. Have a vision. Have a future. Have the time to stop and breathe. Had some lessons to learn. Had some money to earn. Have finally taken control and now it's my fuckin' turn.

Wanted. Want. Want it all. Want it yesterday. Want it hot. Want no dismay. I wanted to be something I was truly not, a bandit only gets the flashy lights, never the jackpot. Want it easy. Want will work for this boy. Want to want things I can have given realistic choice. Want to grow old. Want to try. Want to love like I'm in my prime. Want to be wanted for just being someone at all.

Past and the *present*. It's all been a bit *tense*. Don't look at me for the answers, don't think I'm making sense! But I will say this for times ebb. It's connected like a spider's silken gossamer web. Homeowner or fly is a choice we all get.

Learning to Love

Things are always sweetest in the moment just before, because in the moment after, there's the tiniest of flaws. Like dawn and dusk bring colourful cascades of beauty to our mind, every day. Those days can be long, and the nights can be lonely, sometimes feels like forever in its own little way.

Cherish the illuminating memories that may be found in the annals of our past. Nourish the flourishing of both spirit and soul, allow a heart to grow wings and become fully fledged. Perish the thought of straying from this overgrown, rarely trodden path. Burnished remains the crest you tried to tarnish at the last.

Wondersome wandering, filled with pleasant pondering, sounds like just the ticket to me. Though it has been scant time since a love neared its decline, it appears by fortunate design. Now, in this place and time we could make a life, truly fine. Trying to plant new ideals and grow them like trees.

If you've never truly known the power of a new love's blossoming flower, then unfortunate you truly be. For it inspires when imbibed, a scent that fills the chest with pride. It brings new challenges to personal growth, promotes healthy dialogue and a whole new focus.

It burns brightly like a thousand suns lighting the way, takes your hand softly like moonlight's silver shewn embrace. Emotes laughter that echoes many years later leaving telling lines upon a *goddess's* face. It nestles deep down and makes a home in your bones. Makes you better than your best.

I wrote this for someone with whom I got to fall in love twice. Tried to apply adequate vocabulary and use many a compelling literary device. But I'd swear on my life and know this to be true.

Every Moment I Love You.

What's Good for the Goose
_(2023)_

What's good for the goose is good for the gander; for too long I've allowed this subliminal meander. Never dared to buck against the trend of reeling from disaster to disaster. Body so weary, spent a year in plaster, willing a limb to regenerate faster.

Looked in the mirror and I saw both stranger and ghost, like a parasite showing it's face to its host. When the self loses sight of the path it must follow, all that time you thought you had, turns out it's all borrowed.

But now I'm free from the stake, patting out smouldering flesh. The flames I'd always feared had to burn what was left. Instead of the charred remains, a body lost to the game, you find a natural survivor, this comeback kid's true claim to fame.

You'd think all the blows to the head, sweat-soaked sheets in bed, fleeing the horrifying hordes made of matter and manifested, might have kicked the life from our protagonist; so many agonies alluding to anguish would have laid them down to rest.

But rest is for the dead and, baby, I just started living. Taken so much from this life, perhaps it's time for a little giving. If you're cheating at the game, you're not only cheating the table, you remove the necessity for good intent and honest communication.

Approached with this in mind, it's easy to find next time you seek a reflection in the glass. You can see the whole you but feel brand new, you've changed and you're still standing. Become a powerful force, release self-admonition and remorse, make space for you again.

On the hard days remember the hardships we've handled, reach out for a friend. Share something that matters, helps the dark thoughts to scatter. When you're anxious, have it said. For if we all live in fear, we'll never get these lives in gear, we'll create perfect conditions for a mental pathogen...regret.

So, don't just put it all away, use it to fill up every page, speak it out into the ether, free those animals from their cage. I know life, it comes in stages, and I say this not because I'm sage, but I know what it is to live a life consumed by worthless, worthless rage.

Let it go.

Let it go.

Let it go.

Let. It. Go.

Afterword

Thank you for taking the time to read my life story. It is a work in progress as I'm only about halfway through it. I'm flying on my own now, be it through gales and hurricanes or gentle summer breezes. I'm staying the course and promoting the new me. Perhaps I would liken it to an evolution, like something clicked in the brain of a chimp allowing him to see the task in the macro and use the tools he so crudely made.

I'm using those crude tools to piece back together what I have left. Putting a broken home back together. Patching up damaged relationships. Rebuilding myself piece by painstaking piece. These words I have used for so long flow from a tap in my head that gushes with all the feelings and emotions that could have destroyed me totally. I found a way to use them to my advantage. Hopefully to yours, too.

Nothing in my life has ever been simple, apart from one thing. The simple fact that I was the cause for so much of it all. Had I changed sooner, noticed my slide earlier, maybe we wouldn't be here. Maybe I wouldn't be here. But I am, and if you are there too, then that is always worth fighting for.

Life is ALWAYS worth fighting for.
Love is ALWAYS worth fighting for.
YOU are ALWAYS worth fighting for.

Looks like I had the words after all and there will be more to come. Join us next time for more Husband Material...

"Hardships often prepare ordinary people for an extraordinary destiny."

C.S. Lewis

"Tomorrow is the most important thing in life; it comes to us at midnight very clean. It's perfect when it arrives, and it puts itself in our hands. It hopes we've learned something from yesterday."

John Wayne

"I have learned over the years that when one's mind is made up, this diminishes fear."

Rosa Parks

Index
Title and First Lines Arranged Chronologically

A

Another father tells lies and two little girls cry..., 50

B

Battlefield, 72
Battlefields of history lay scattered with our dead..., 72
Bird vs. Person, 48

C

Captain and The Lover, The, 19
crazy like the glue but my bonds don't always stick, I'm, 28

D

Demons, 43
Digging Bones, 45
Dog Knight, The, 55
Drinks served on the bar of the Titanic II, remind me of a time when..., 19

E

eaten food like a fiend and drank myself into bitter, I've…, 16
Even with no strings attached…, 59
Ever felt like walking on a tightrope…, 61

F

Fables from the Storm, 70
Father please I beg of you…, 43
Foil, Toil, Trouble on the Boil, 31
For the Bairns, 50

H

Had naught, so give me crosses…, 77
Hard to be a hero when filled with malicious intent…, 55
Hold the line for your life, hold the line for your money…, 34

I

It's All Getting a Bit Tense, 81
It was seven thirty on a night in ninety-six…, 40

K

known downs and I've known pick-me-ups, I've…, 45

L

Learning to Love, 83
Loss. Lost. Lost the plot, 81

M

Many moons have passed but many moons I spent sitting on the edge…, 24
Monstrous Machine, 17
monstrous machine greased and oiled by the crooked regime, The…, 17

O

On Hold, 34
Overachieving Disbeliever, 13

P

Packing up Promises, 52

Q

Queen and Country, 18

Queens to Me, 59

S

Seven Thirty, 37
Sitting surrounded by a life that could truly have been yours…, 52
Small Gods. Big Problems, 77
Sometimes a soul may escape through a hole, a decimal point…, 31
Spent too long wrapped up in the past like Alice staring into the…, 63
Suits You, 63

T

Things are always sweetest in the moment just before…, 83
Thirteen Miles, 75
This is a recitation by a national treasure…, 48
thought that storms were caused by static, I…, 70
Tightrope, 61
Times are for trains and I'm off the tracks, late to the station…, 32
Today we received, overachieved and I see yet, we still disbelieve in…, 13
Transport is a Pain, 32

V

Vampiric Pen, 16
VietDan, 28

W

What's Good for the Goose, 85
What's good for the goose is good for the gander…, 85
What's it come to when the Queen is almost dead, and the country…, 18
When did this crown become my iron mask? 75
World Wor, 24

About The Author

D.L. Husband

D.L. 'Dan' Husband is a thirty-five-year-old writer and hospitality worker, lifelong North Easterner and living currently in the County Durham area.
A die-hard fan of both literature and football (Newcastle United 'til I die).

When he is not working or writing, he will be reading or listening to audiobooks, spending time with his partner, Emily, and rutting around the North East looking for performance and publishing opportunities, to add to this dream come true of pursuing writing as a primary focus more and more.

Please follow him @husbandmaterialpoetryandprose on Instagram for all this and a bit of that.

Printed in Great Britain
by Amazon